BRILLIANT LITTLE BODY

Brett Elizabeth Jenkins

Riot in Your Throat
publishing fierce, feminist poetry

Jenkins, Brett Elizabeth.
1st edition.
ISBN: 979-8-9889898-0-6

Cover Art: Beth Madeley
Cover Design: Kirsten Birst
Book Design: Shanna Compton
Author Photo: Brett Elizabeth Jenkins

Riot in Your Throat
Arlington, VA
www.riotinyourthroat.com

I love the body. Flesh is so honest, and organs do not lie.
Terri Guillemets

In short, I wanted to know what I was.
Adolphe Monod

CONTENTS

A MAN IN AN ILLINOIS TOLLBOOTH CALLED ME A 'BEAUTIFUL WOMAN' AS I WAS DRIVING AWAY

and I turned my car around, jumped into
his small sanctuary, and started a family there
in that dirty box. We subsist on nickels and rubber
gloves, snips of song lyrics pouring out of sedan
windows. *Now, love, love don't come easy. But
I keep on waiting, anticipating for that soft voice . . .*

You're a beautiful woman he told me, and now we live
in this toll booth collecting coins. Our seven children
tap dance on the median. We sleep in a pile like puppies.
They don't go to school, but we don't get in trouble
because the police are scared of our strange family.
Windows open and shut. I'm beautiful. We have all this.

MY MOTHER PRAYS FOR ME IN 1986 AND IT GOES HORRIBLY AWRY

In the year of my birth, my mother went to mass
and prayed for me—that I would never go hungry.
That I would always be healthy. That I would not
end up a rodeo clown. She asked around
and, on average, 49.5 rodeo clowns are trampled
every year by bulls. And besides, have terrible
benefits. Instead, I ended up a sad poet.
What did she expect? I fritter away
my meager earnings on beer and nail polishes
with names like "Unicorn Puke" and "Shake
Your Money Maker." I have had strange jobs—
I worked in a factory that made aluminum cans.
One summer I sold fish to rich snobs.
I don't believe in God, but maybe
he answered my mother's prayer.
I can imagine my life as a rodeo clown, married
to a stout matador, living in our RV and traveling
from city to city performing for drunk honky-tonk
dads and truck driving chain-smokers.
It's not a glamorous life, but people laugh
when I pull down my pants to show my bloomers,
and my husband has only been gored twice.

BEFORE WE WERE EX-LOVERS

we were moon-drunk on each other—
nesting in caves of bedsheets, sharing
cans of Miller High Life in dim lit corners.
Before we were moon-drunk on each other
we were timid foxes, hand-holding in slight rain, headlights
vanishing before us in early dusk while we smoked
Parliaments on stoops. If time is a loop, there is still some
place in me where your neck smells like fireplace
and aftershave, our first record spinning groggily
in the corner of a dirty apartment. There is still a place
where we sit in a vinyl booth at Maria's and order eggs
and toast on a snow day, a place where
we trudge home in our thrifted boots
and put on Dylan while the sun lights up the white
patches outside the window.
If there is a place, it's where my small bones sink
in next to yours on the first bed we bought—
where now I listen for jays
in the mornings, alone—the same place.

WHEN NON-POETS ASK ME WHAT MY POEMS ARE ABOUT

I usually just say *murder*. I don't write about murder
(at least not exclusively) but there is no good way
to tell them, baby, you're looking at it. My poems
are about my hair, about the way it's been unwashed
since last Friday but I'll still let you run your fingers through it
if you buy me four White Claws and say I'm pretty.
My poetry is about the moon, of course,
because she's the only fucking rock in our sky—
even space real estate prices are outrageous.
We've just met at this bar and there's no easy way
to slide into a conversation about the winter
I fell through the ice, the dreams I have
about the fog-raked lakes. Every time I forget
to put my turn signal on, it's a poem, and the time
an old woman flipped me off while wearing mittens,
that was certainly a poem. My poems arrive
in Uber Eats bags almost every Monday evening,
and my bumper sticker that says *horses aren't real*
is a poem. I got a big poem the year I failed
religion class, the same year I learned how
to choose a shade of concealer that's just right for me—
porcelain white. My poems wear t-shirts they found
on the side of the road, and they drive
two and a half hours to leave flowers on gravestones.
In the morning, I wake up and open the curtains
to hear if the poems are chirping—they usually are.
The old adage says a rotten apple spoils the whole barrel,
but my poems just cut off the bad part
and use the rest to make cider. I'm not afraid
to eat mold or fall down in the dirt or get caught

dancing in the supermarket, and I'm not afraid
to write about murder, so when I answer your question,
I'm not really lying, but no, I'm not telling the whole truth, either.

I KNOW SOMETHING ABOUT LOVE

I too saw the movie *Love Actually* in college
and made subsequent poor decisions related to dating.
I know how to wring my hands in the dark
and drink too much wind and fall down dumb
in the grass, laughing. The laughing never lasts
but what does is white-hot and breaks you
into a sweat at night. I know something about love.
I know the patterns the rain makes in the gutters
and those night noises you make when you turn over
under the sheets. I know how to wait for loss.
I know how to find the other shoe and drop it.

I COME FROM THESE BODIES

—women shucking corn on wooden porch stoops,
       their men drinking Busch Light

around the dingy glow of the television.
       Knotted hands scratching down

lottery numbers, same time each Friday.
       One small lake in Minnesota

where I thought I might drown
       and wanted to. The moon's glint

off the windshield of the white minivan I crashed
       one November and designs drawn in my palm

on a schoolyard, meant to keep away evil.
       When I was small, I was carried sleeping

out of my grandparents' house. I was small enough
       to be buoyed between two arms, draped across

the backseat of a Buick Skyhawk. Of course
       I live there too—in that second between

wakefulness and dreaming where I'm small again,
       capable of anything.

In the sleepy moments
       I'm unaware of love.

THE PROBLEM OF THE BODY

And since there is no solution to the problem
of the body, it's possible the next best thing
is to walk through tall weeds. Swim out
to the center of the lake at dusk, the stars
just beginning to glitter. Science says
the end result will always be that we are separated
from our bodies. But while we have them,
it's best to throw them into unmade beds
and get them drunk on gin and tonic.
Little impossible body, I want to have
counted all the crows you've seen
and all the times you fell to your knees.
Counted how many doors you have opened,
calculate the area of skin covered
by kisses. If there is no solution to the body,
give it variables. Introduce it to tall
redheaded boys on a Thursday evening.
Pour whiskey into the system.
Catalog its dreams. Put it dead-tired
on its feet under the moon
and see what happens.

AN EXPERT'S GUIDE TO CHAOS

Chaos is easy   but you need to be born
      into a family with a drunk

        Find stillness
    in the moments between   The theory goes
random or seemingly unpredictable behavior
        in systems
is still governed   by deterministic

    laws   If you leave fingerprints
        on the hallway mirror
he will get drunk
         If you fail religion class
           he will get drunk   If you say
damn
        during dinner   he will get drunk

    If you forget to feed the dog   he will
get drunk   then kill the dog

      When you leave the little house
on Erie Street   you notice that the chaos has crept

      into your body
It pulls your bedroom
    out of orbit

Your body   a little brilliant machine
      You give it booze

to keep it right   that's part
              of the algorithm

        One pinch of Lithium   a dash
of sleep   But because
you are an expert
        you know that an object   in chaos
stays in chaos
            There's nothing to be done

POEM ABOUT WIND

Here we go. This poem is about wind.
The way you can't see it but know it's there
like last summer's heartbreak—the nights
you spent reciting facts about Jupiter
to yourself in bed, trying to sleep. It's true
you can't see heartache, only the byproducts of it—

lying on the floor pretending to be dead,
the dishes piling up in the sink. But this poem
is about wind, I said, how it's the only one
to open your door. The miracle of a leaf
tornado in the Walgreens parking lot,
and you alone to see it. The way the wind

pushes dark clouds into your stomach
and you swallow them without question.
When the wind turns up at your stoop
it says, *blah blah blah* but you know
that's code for *I have felt the face of every
dead person you've ever loved.* This is a problem.

The wind obviously has the upper hand.
Yes, the wind pushes ocean water, it moves
your mom's hair in that photo from 1982—
the wind is in every photo.
How something invisible can make me feel
so small and unwanted. Just like that.

MARRYING THE WIND

I proposed to the wind and the wind said yes
but now we are encountering extreme difficulties

putting together our wedding registry.
The wind wants feathers, dust bunnies,

confetti. It has no interest in candelabras. The wind
wants only things that can be carried

on its soft voice. I want all the seasons
of *Breaking Bad*. The wind cannot appreciate

Walter White, but it may like to carry away a cloud
of smoke. I am unsure if my love can be held

in the wind's arms. Nothing is softer than the wind's arms—
it loves to hold hands with my hair. But I want to fight

about this espresso machine the wind doesn't want.
The wind cannot pick up the registry scanner

so I am forced to do all the booping.
Cornmeal *boop*. Flour *boop*. Wood shavings *boop*.

I buy a Diet Coke and the wind takes the receipt.
I scream into the wind and the wind screams back.

OUR HAPPINESS

The gray veil of November had come
down. We, both a little sad at the ebbs
of life, lay in your bed entangled
in the rumpled orange comforter.
We were both shirtless, the window
open, the cool air coming in to sanitize
our sadness. My head in the crook
of your body. You were telling me
about the hot air balloon craze
in the Romantic period, how a man
had fallen from a height of two hundred
feet into a freshly plowed field. The man's
legs buried themselves in the earth
up to his waist and the force of the impact
made his organs explode out into a neat
red circle surrounding his body. We lay there
for a time considering this, embracing.

IN THIS UNIVERSE

Everyone lives in a trailer park. The trailers are lined up
one after another like spectacular dominoes,
and they all look just the same. We all come from
the wrong side of the tracks. We all run barefoot
over stones and eat potatoes from a box.
There are no Ryans or Bryans, no football captains
to make fun of my lot number. There are no lot numbers—
there's just a big party in the field at the end
of the horseshoe near the sign that says Young's
Suburban Estates where we light a fire and the littlest,
blondest girl swings and lets out a yell that sounds
like a wind chime. We all bury our dead pets in the cornfield
across the road. We still get sad in this heaven,
but the neighbors show up with a casserole dish
and never ask for it back. The clouds move more gently
over this universe of only trailers. Everyone's
gardens stay watered, and the mailman knows
all our names. We go on like this. We could go on like this.

FAILED HAIKU

this is how to survive/ any given Thursday/ dress yourself in houndstooth & feathers/ walk quietly & resolutely/ toward the edge of the path/ this is how to carry the dead/ burn your old diaries/ in the cornfield behind your childhood home &/ wait for the wind to pick up the ashes/ carry them with it down to Albuquerque/ this is how to survive/ if you're drowning/ stay calm/ breathe naturally/ & keep kicking/ don't think about the winter you fell/ beneath the river ice/ as a young girl/ green coat soaked/ dad mad as a hatter/ this is another way to survive/ & another/ but I won't tell you what they are/ I will tell you/ you should not be afraid of death/ even though it makes sense to be afraid/ which is to say/ freak out if you feel like it/ this is how to freak out/ buy three bottles of wine/ & drink them in the parking lot/ of the church you attended as a child/ knock on the door of the parsonage/ don't worry/ he won't answer/ it's three in the morning/ this is what you do next/ pass out in your neighbor's car/ & wake up in your childhood bed/ then drive to the river where/ you almost drowned/ & skip stones until you get one/ with six skips/ think about it sinking/ to the bottom/ your feet/ plunging through the ice/ & stop wishing/ it were still you

BENIGN LITTLE LIFE

Before the days of drinking
boxed wine alone in my bath towel,
I was married. At 24, we stood
in front of 75 people & told them
we'd love each other forever,
which was half a lie.
We lived in shitty apartments
with landlords named Terry
or Jerry & we ate cheap rice &
drove dogshit cars, but for a while
we were happy, I think,
huddling close to each other
in the cold months like small animals.
But maybe I have never been happy
or don't know how to quantify
these mercurial sensations
of the body—these misbehaving machines
we live in. How we could have gone on
together—a benign little life—& been
just fine had one of us not left.
& I'm glad it didn't have to be me.

ALMOST CHA-CHA

I tell people that when I was born, my mother
was on drugs and so she named me Brett.
But what I don't tell them is that she almost
named me Charlotte and wanted to call me
Cha-Cha. My almost-name seeps with sugar
and sequins, a ballet dancer with a nicotine
patch slapped over a half-sleeve tattoo
of a big-tittied mermaid with a fu manchu.
If I were Cha-Cha, I swear to god I'da had

all the boys in my sixth-grade class smoking
Parliaments with me under the bleachers.
Ryan Goldstein woulda never knocked the books
out of my hands, and the girls would've lined up
at my locker to get a look at my new Chuck Taylors.
My mama would have wanted to rename me
in high school when I started going god-knows-
where at two in the morning with Jason Wheeler,
knocking back Miller High Lifes and throwing

the cans at speeding trains. Cha-Cha is my id,
the girl in the purple dress at the funeral.
The hot-lipped, fuck-you-very-much fast talker
selling fake IDs out the back of her pop-up camper.
In my dreams I'm her, a goddess in ruin, a red
lipstick, denim jacket pool shark with a taste
for whiskey. Who don't take no shit. Who lets
the cares of this world slip through her hands
like air, like dust, like something impossible to hold.

PIONEERS

we in young love own the school, walk around in denim jackets like fuck you
we in love in pickup trucks kiss with cigarette lips
in love, we exchange Vonnegut books like
we are the first, we have discovered him
we have discovered love, we bump our bodies together
our bodies, together, we tattoo and drink
we roll into the night
in the night in our young love, we are pioneers of the road
we so in love drape our bodies against pinball machines and in diner booths
in diner booths we coffee and sigh
so in love we sing tom petty on balconies when the power goes out
we slip out of windows in the full moon to kiss against bricks
in love, in love, we have everything to lose and we don't care

I HAVE SOMETHING TO TELL THE BODY

My beloved little body, intractable machine,
you small living clock—I have something to tell you
but I don't know what it is. If there is a God,
I ask that he look the other way while I fill you
with carbohydrates & something called maltodextrin.
While I soak you in the giant puddles of the earth.
Yes, bag of blood, we are the body
in this poem. We're not separate. I don't understand
the science, but somehow the I & the you
are mixed up—cocktailed together, little breakable
system. One day I figure you will have had enough
& give up. But which one of us will be to blame,
pale container? How surprised we should all be
that we keep the same body our whole life,
the things that happen to it like icons on a map.
Where do my country summer days live,
my middle school love for murder books?
What happened to the place
in my breastbone where I loved violently
a tall man in a raincoat? God,
if you're there, put me in a boat
& make me feel small & hungry, one drop
of water in a galactic raincloud.

MY WRITING TEACHER ASKS ME TO WRITE ABOUT SOMETHING BAD I DID

and I have twenty minutes to do it. I ask
whether I can have an extra six weeks to complete
the assignment. You see the thing is, I was born
on a Thursday and was primed for this exercise.
I was born with six bad decisions ready to go.
One of those decisions was marrying
a literature major. The rest of those decisions
came out ten years later asking for White Claw.
Give us your poor, your tired, your hungry
adjunct professors huddled at the foot
of a Tinder date gone wrong. My writing teacher
asks me to write about something bad I did
and I turn in my birth certificate. I turn in
my college transcripts, with a C- in theology
because the day I showed up to give a presentation
on St. Paul I was hungover and puked all over
the slide projector. I didn't pick up the phone
when she called, and she jumped from the bridge
hours later. I've xeroxed my butt in exactly four states.
I have forgotten my first address. I have given
my ATM pin code to a first date. I'm not sure,
but I think my underpants are at the bottom
of at least two lakes in Vermont. I have done things
I regret. I have regrets I could alphabetize.
I will make more. I still think of her.

TEN OF SWORDS

After ten years together you call me from four
hundred miles away to tell me you're going in search
of some other hunger. I feel each year pierce me
back to front—the years trace my spine like a solemn,
slow arpeggio. I don't know what I'm doing, don't know
I'm trying to jump from the car until my mother pulls over
in the parking lot of a Perkins, follows me into the grass
and tries to hold me. I'm pressed by the weight of this
marriage, lifted away from me. How can something taken
away feel so heavy? How can I weigh anything at all?

THE MAGICIAN'S HANDBOOK

Never pull anything out of your hat—
that is for amateurs and children's birthday parties.

If you must cut someone in half,
think of your ex-lovers. In particular,

the smell of them in the morning
when the sheets were still damp with sweat.

Guard your pocketbook, and never give away
gum. People who ask for gum are always

willing to take more. All your superstitions
are vault-heavy and real as rust. Do not deny yourself

these small prayers. If you must reach into your hat,
let it be to conceal your fist,

whether you are hiding it in anger or you have
stolen something very small. You may

from time to time need to convince someone
they haven't heard what they have just heard.

Misdirect. Move on. Always remember that you
are the true trick and you must never reveal yourself.

Not to anyone, not even the moon.

PRAYER, IN WINTER

The sun is still up. But when it goes down,
Insoluble God, is when the questions pour
out like water. What of the next world—
and will there be poplar trees?
Are my dreams a reckoning of sorts?
The man with the fucked-up ear I see
at the bus stop—will he be okay? What
will happen, and why did I do what I did?
I don't ask for any want of answer—
what comes is only the small hum
of the refrigerator, the wind-whip
of the branch as a blue jay leaves
for 38th Street. Unreachable God,
there is just one thing I need,
and I don't know what it is.

DIVORCE

In the night I wonder—is there just one
moment when the milk goes bad?
Is it safe to drink one moment
and not the next? And where did we
go so wrong? For years, our toothbrushes
neatly hugging each other in their cup.
Me, knotting the loose noose
of a half Windsor around your neck
for a New Year's party. Pick
your moment. These or any before
or after. The ones we sat soundless
on the couch for the pizza
to arrive. Even the ones laughing
deep into the onyx-shaded night,
sitting on the stoop
with a glass of wine, a crooked smile,
your hand draped over your knee
like a dead man's. We had
already begun to go bad.

LAST NIGHT I DREAMED

I bought you fruit. No one else
was in the grocery store, just me picking out
the ripest pears and firmest Honeycrisp
apples for you to feast on. When I awoke
I called my mom and asked her
what the dream meant. She said *Honey,*
it's obviously all those years of Bible training.
Don't you know you're not supposed
to fornicate? You're bein' FedEx'd to hell
and you ain't even know it. I woke up again
to find that this was a dream within a dream
(I should have known—I never call people)
and texted you to tell you about what my mom said.
We agreed that later you would come over
and you'd fornicate me. I thought back
to all my years of Bible learning
and remembered when Adam and Eve
got kicked out of the garden of Eden
they were ashamed of being naked
and so maybe I wouldn't go to hell
for my fornicating if only I just wasn't ashamed
of being naked, so I took off all my clothes
and went into the backyard to hang up the bedsheets.
My neighbors were in their backyard too,
having a birthday party. They wanted to know
just what I was doing. They asked me,
Just what are you doing?
I told them, *Getting ready to fornicate,*
and I went back inside
while my bedsheets dried in the wind.

IN THE MIDDLE OF THE NIGHT I WAKE UP TO PEE

having drunk my weight in hard seltzers and gin
the night before. As I sit down on the cold
toilet seat I think about my mom asking me
a few weeks ago if I value my life.
Of course not. My head is fuzzy, and I consider
the word *value*, as if my life were worth
a month's paycheck. As a thirty-five-year-old
poet turned teaching assistant turned
quasi-alcoholic, the value of my life is depreciating.
I have peeled tangerines with these thumbs
for three decades, felt the soft powder of their skins
coat my fingers like I have crawled
through the dust on my hands and knees
looking for water.
The ends of my hair have seen years. Seen snow
from Minneapolis balconies. I wonder
if the longest part of my hair was with me
during my marriage that ended
four years ago, wonder how many hands
have touched it. I flush the toilet
and take a cool drink from the faucet, water
coating the downy hair on my face.
I am sixty percent water. And water touches everything.
There must be some value in that.

HYPOTHESIS

One day, something will be different. But not today,
when I only have one heart and it's full of this year's
sadness—the oranges going bad on the counter,

and the numbers of ex-lovers rotting in my phone.
Oh, body, we were made for something, but not this.
Not the recurring dream we have where our teeth

crumble like plaster. Not small towns with names
like Kingsport or Clyde. And we certainly
weren't made for the impossible way the stars shine

over high school football fields like it's nothing.
And on some unnoteworthy Monday, we'll die—
face-down in a doorway or choking down an apology

in front of the friends we have left. But body,
we did it together—joined at some ghostly hinge—
and when I'm gone, they'll put you away.

And I suppose that's when things will be different.

THIRTEEN THINGS YOU REALLY NEED TO KNOW ABOUT ME

1. I don't know shit about basketball. Gonzaga
   sounds like a cheese to me.

2. I once boosted a copy
   of *The Rime of the Ancient Mariner*
   from my college library. It's the only thing
   I've ever stolen.

3. When I was thirteen, I drank one beer
   with Nikki Vassello in her dad's basement
   and pretended to be drunk.
   I definitely was not.

4. My favorite sound in the world
   is the THX movie opening sound.

5. My friend's dad once shamed me
   about how infrequently I flossed my teeth
   and I want bad things to happen to him.

6. When you say *bless you* after I sneeze
   I never say thank you back, and it's not
   because I don't like you. It's because
   I just don't care about being alive.

7. Last week, I told my cat I liked her beard
   but she didn't respond.

8. After about five Michelob Golden Lights
   I'll play anyone in pool and lose badly.

9. I'll pony up the money if they ask.

10. I've been the person crying
    in the bathroom at the bar.

11. My friend just told me she's trying hard
    not to meet any new people this year.

12. My mom wants me to stop writing
    so many sad poems, but I'll probably
    still be sad either way.

13. Last week my therapist asked me
     how I was doing, and I told him,
     the Earth is spinning rapidly on its axis,
     He shrugged and said, *I guess.*

REASONS I'VE CRIED

Because I've spent so many March nights
looking at the moon alone, shitfaced in my underwear.
Because what the fuck is up with all that stuff
with King David and Bathsheba?
Because I can't talk to my cat. Because I got a 32%
on a midterm and my professor wrote "ouch"
on the top of my paper. Because I purposely bought
a single mango White Claw for myself
on a bad day and dropped it in the parking lot
where it exploded. Believe it or not,
I've cried because I realized I felt happy
for the first time in weeks.
I've cried in the Target checkout line
buying pregnancy tests and in the dentist's office
getting a root canal. I once cried in French class
after forgetting the word for *heart*
(it's *cœur*). I could be crying right now for all you know.
I've cried over TikTok videos and TV shows
and when my best friend died, I cried for three days straight
and had to drink Gatorade to replenish my electrolytes.
I've been sugarsad and winterweepy.
And of course I've thought my sadness was big enough
to have other, smaller sadnesses orbit it.
But today I noticed the grass is suddenly green
and I rolled down the car windows
and heard trains doing the things that trains do.
I watched the sun make its slow trek
down the far part of the sky, and I smell faintly
of campfire, and I am not crying, and I don't want
to be crying, but we'll see what tomorrow holds.

AFTER TEN YEARS MY HUSBAND LEAVES ME TO 'FIND HIMSELF'

I say, I'm sorry I can't understand what you're saying.
I turn the radio down. I say, pull over
into the parking lot of this Perkins. I say,
where do you think your self went.
I say, you sure have read a lot of Nietzsche.
I say, my-my-my. I say it's hopeless as holding
a bag of strawberries in the rain. I say a lot of things
and he turns his head softly from side to side
like a depressed oscillating fan. I lift my hands
to my face. I'm not sure where the sun went.
I say has there always been a giant fire burning
itself in the sky like a question. He doesn't answer.
I say answer me. He walks out to the end
of the Perkins parking lot and we sit in the grass.
I say this is nice grass for a Perkins. I say how long
have you known. He says yes. I say you know
we'll have to split up our books
and he says I can have them all.

THERE IS NO OTHER PERSON IN THIS POEM

I have a special outfit I put on when I'm sad.
I call it Jim.

I get sad when I think about how close dream
& doom live to each other—

just two houses apart—& when I remember
the old bank from the town where I grew up.

There's an earsplitting loneliness to this life—
the way you can wonder alone

at the gibberish of a river &
nobody will know it. How the sun dries

the ocean salt to your arms & legs but
no one else thinks about it.

I did this to myself.
There is no other person in this poem.

I could have made up anything
to make me less lonely, but here I am again

writing about how sad I am.
What is sadness, anyway & why does it smell

like pine trees & whiskey?
Why does it take its shoes off when it arrives,

knowing I will ask it to stay?

ABSENCE

It isn't true about the heart.
As far as absence is concerned,
it turns the heart to stone.
The heart walks the fields
at night past abandoned barns,
the old doors yawned open—
nothing kept secret.
The moon sees everything
and writes it down in her diary.
One sad heart
flitting through the wildflowers.
Another moving softly
from one room to another,
sometimes singing.
The thing about stone hearts
is the moon becomes their mother.
She draws them to the water
thinks of them often
wants to cook for them.
But like most moons
she has no arms—no way
to hold a thing. I am not
a daughter of the sun.
The night knows me and my business.

LESSONS

When life gives you lemons, cry and say you really, really don't want them.

When life gives you lemons, lie on the floor and pretend to be dead.

When life gives you lemons, huddle in the corner with your sister and tell knock-knock jokes until the sun comes up.

When life gives you lemons, don't come up to the surface too quickly or you could get the bends.

When life doesn't go as planned, it's best to eat cheese about it.

When an invasive plant grows in your backyard, pluck it and put it in old spaghetti jars with a little water in the bottom. Give it to your neighbor so they'll bake a pie for you.

When your neighbor bakes you a pie, share it with your other neighbor—the one with the messed-up fingers—because she's been in a bad mood and maybe it's from lack of pie.

When life throws you a curveball, don't swing. The next one might hit you and you can walk to first base without having to do any heavy lifting.

When your grandma tells you not to get drunk before they call the lottery numbers, that's a lesson worth remembering.

When I'm dead and gone, I want people to say, man I bet that girl took out her recycling.

When I die, scatter me in my hometown, but don't cremate me first.

When I'm gone, when I'm really good and dead, tell them I did what I could.

When the sun goes down over my last day, it won't even know.

SEVEN THINGS

1.
Don't get drunk
when it's a full moon.
Or do. What do I know?

2.
It's fair to say that I have struggled
to love my life—or even, at times,
like it—the heavy July days spent
under sweat-damp sheets,
heat lightning opening
the corners of the room.

3.
When you know something
will pain you terribly,
but you do it anyway, is there
a word for this?
If so, it lives in my breast pocket.

4.
When you get down-and-out sad,
you might need to print out
a Mary Oliver poem
and eat it.
Or call your mom if you don't have a printer.

5.
At night I pray to the patron saint
of rest stop bathrooms

and ask him to intercede for me—
for the terrible things I've done.
I figure he probably doesn't get
many prayers, so maybe
he can fit me in quick.

6.
The idea of happiness is like the knife
I use to open my medical bills.

7.
It's wild we get this one small life
and have to live it end to end.
Wherever that is.

HOW GORILLA GLUE COULDN'T SAVE MY MARRIAGE

When I got married, my friend
got me a gift certificate to Williams & Sonoma.
I used it to buy a butter dish, a bread knife,
and some fancy cheese I didn't end up liking.
Two years later, she jumped
off a bridge in Boston into the Mystic River.
A few years later, my husband broke
the handle off the butter dish,
and then he left me, too. He didn't break
the butter dish on purpose, but I think about it
all the time—the way he used Gorilla Glue
to put the knob back on after I threw
myself on the kitchen floor, crying.
It's just a butter dish, he said, and he wasn't wrong,
I guess, but he was. If it's stupid
to have an emotional attachment
to a butter dish, that's okay.
But I've loved it longer
than my husband could love me,
so you decide what that means.

THERE ARE BIRDS IN THIS POEM

And of course there are. What self-respecting poet
has a poem without a bird in it, or a woman hungering
after a man she can never have?
The birds are probably woodpeckers
because they are loyal and begin courtship
in deep winter, which has to mean something
really powerful for this poem, I think.
This poem also has trees in it—pines, maybe,
or oaks. Something that lets you know the poet
grew up in Ohio and subtly hints
at a long history of mental illness.
Is spruce the tree I'm looking for?
No matter. This poem has other cool features,
like a dog who has gone three days without food,
and the moon, of course, cracking its dull light
like an egg over a small Indiana town.
But at the heart of this poem is a girl who has nothing—
not even an em dash—looking for a way out.
A way to spin her heartache as a joke. A reason
to see herself as the hero and not the person who fucks
everything up. A girl who wants, at the end of the day,
to be the bird in this poem. How small. How light.

FIRST MAY IN FORT WAYNE AFTER FINALLY GETTING MY MEDS ADJUSTED BY MY PSYCHIATRIST

In mid-May I sit quietly on the back porch
with my neighbor, watching birds dart
between telephone poles.
The yard next door reminds me of a puzzle

my mom did the summer of 1998
and I want each day to be this sort of slow—
white wine slow, mess of sparrows
congregating in the driveway slow.

I want the smell of freshly cut grass
to haunt me in the winter months, and I want
my days to build up one on top of another
like a book whose author has lost track

of the plot. I want to be surprised
by the arrival of fall, and I want to call my sister
and tell her when I forget
the word for *toaster*. I want to feel weightless

in the ocean after eating too many potato chips
in the sand. Sorry to get like this
(I'm not, actually) but it's mid-May
and I have this impossible feeling.

THE NEXT DAY

I'm in bed in a new city I don't love. Last night a man pulled me
into his car and pinned me down.

His breath smelled of cheap beer and desperation.
I could not get away. Since then,

I have been in bed in a city I don't love.
All my ex-lovers are six hundred and forty-seven miles

away, going about their daily tasks—
taking the bills out of the mailbox.

Picking up groceries from Target. In this strange
and blue-gray moment, I miss each one of them.

How they handled the terrible question
of my body. The things they said

in the pitch of night. I want
to walk back into that old body.

Have that body walk its way to me—
all six hundred and forty-seven miles. Lay its hands

on the half-moon of my stomach. Tell this new body
it did nothing wrong.

SUNDAY AFTERNOONS

Because Sundays are not sad enough,
I have specific rituals to make them more sad.
Afternoons, I lie in bed and think of ex-lovers.
The days we traipsed through co-ops
picking out oranges, considering the wobble
and heft of them. I take out the hats
they left in my apartment to see
if there is any whiff of them there.
On days that feel particularly
too happy, I make a point to drive by
Brian's home to see if I can catch
a glimpse of him with his fiancée,
who just got her hair cut a few weeks ago
(it's darling). John's apartment
is especially easy to get into.
I like to monitor his mail—I can usually
tell how he's doing by how many
Amazon boxes arrive at his stoop
monthly. It pains me to do these things,
but I know they must be done.
Sunday is when Alex takes out his recycling.
He's been drinking too much
and I really do worry for him.
I think he's got a problem.

WAYS TO DIE

Show me a girl
who's walked home from the bar
alone & I'll show you a girl

who's thought about
every conceivable way to die.
Dragged

into a hot dog factory &
put in the meat grinder. Guts
chopped up & used as piano strings.

Bricked up into the basement
of an abandoned building.
At night, she dreams of being hog-tied

& put under false panels
in a white van, driven down the highway &
across the border—sold

to the highest-bidding cartel.
She wakes up in her bed, the smell
of dirt & lime

still lingering in her nostrils.
Everyone knows a girl is disposable.
Made to be crumpled

like a wet paper towel. Nobody knows
that the girl in this poem
is me &

that girl is a river.
She travels swiftly & never stops,
not even

when she reaches her destination.
If you stop, you're caught &
if you're caught, you're dead.

OTHER POSSIBLE LIVES

When I was born, my small shaky body
traveled a path down an inexhaustible road:

did not die when hit on her pink Huffy
in front of her childhood home,

did not die when she crashed through the river ice
one January evening, alone under the white stars

of Orion's Belt. I could have led these bones down
any number of alternate paths—could have become

a nun and offered my body to the caverns of a convent
or run off with the redhead Jason Henry in tenth grade

to make bombs in the woods and live off the land.
In one life it's like a spot the differences puzzle—

just the gray cat is missing, a tattoo I never got,
and a few more scars. One of my favorites

has me living in a small Norwegian hut surrounded by chickens.
Yes, there are many paths where I'm dead—

ones where they've laid my body down, covered in white
flowers. Ones where I was sixteen, twenty,

thirty-six. These are other possible lives.
But it's this one where I'm made to live, this still-

warm chest, this small attic apartment,
this fireplace, and the days going by like dark trains.

MODEL VILLAGE

When I was seventeen, I climbed
the only water tower in my town and looked out
over all the fog-lonely houses.

The human animal is such a strange creature,
my friend once told me—
what are we all out here doing?

Why do we congregate in small towns,
pray to small gods? We don't know
what else to do. We cut class to get high

at the reservoir. We make up little stories
about the foxes who live in the woods
behind our house. Sometimes

we sell all our shit and move to Chicago.
At the top of the water tower,
my town looked like the model village

from the movie *Beetlejuice*. But it was real.
The people in were it watching
Monday Night Football and heating up

Hungry-Man dinners. How strange
this place seemed from up there—
how ethereal and small.

If there is a god, I pray
he puts his thumb over the whole earth
and snubs us out.

PARTY TRICKS FOR A SAD POET

1. Swim out as far as you can into the lake beside your mom's old house. Tread water until you think you will drown. Wait for someone to notice you.

2. Tell your therapist about the dream you've been having—the one where you're trapped somewhere & trying to scream for help but can't make any noise.

3. Drink three bottles of wine. That's the whole trick. Look how you float.

4. In the bath, imagine you are a Victorian widow.

5. When your lover tells you not to walk home from the bar alone, do it anyway—imagine it's your last night alive. Notice the smell of chamomile bushes in the alley outside your apartment. Breathe in deep.

6. Forget your mother's maiden name.

7. Walk quietly to the edge of a cliff. Take off your shoes. Think about magic.

8. Buy a telescope to spy on your neighbors. Barbara is sleeping with the fish salesman from Acorn Street. Again.

9. Disappear for a while. Get in your car and drive to South Dakota. Fake a British accent in the bar to weasel free drinks out of the locals. Move in with Bud, who owns a trailer home near James River.

10. The most important trick to learn is to be quiet. Stand stone-still at the back of a party and watch people lean against one another—fall helplessly in love.

OCTOBER COMES TO DINNER

October has the fucking audacity to come again this year—
a scheduled heartbreak.
She's wearing an ostentatious orange blazer & knocking
on my door with the persistence
of a Bible salesman. She comes inside & we light a fire.
October brings her own tea.
My grandma always told me that October has answers,
so I show her my body
and ask her questions about it. Can I feel safe in here?
Can I feel at home here?
October doesn't give me any answers. She comes with me
as I go about my day.
We buy lunch meat at Kroger & schedule a visit
with my therapist.
October accompanies me to session. My therapist
seems unfazed
that October has taken up residence in the room—
he doesn't mention her at all
& I become agitated. I leave & she's still following me
like a dog who knows
my condition is terminal. I ask her again—
can I feel safe in here?
Can I feel at home here? We go on like this
for thirty-one days:
taking naps together, touching each leaf in the backyard,
killing them.
October's sun makes its last disappearance &
she pulls me onto the porch.
We drink wine together. I ask her again—can I feel safe in here?

Can I feel at home here?
She goes to the door to leave & I say *not yet*.
She says I have my answer.

AUTUMN IN FORT WAYNE

The leaves are doing their yearly duty of giving up
real estate on the ends of branches
and I'm getting all weird and nostalgic—
thinky—because I'm a poet and was born
with a wandering heart. The small questions
must be asked in the quiet hours of the morning
when the birds are just rising from their nests
and you have not yet fallen asleep
because you're staring at the moon coming
in through the blinds, touching the face of a man
you said the word *love* to yesterday.
Yes, love. I know we said that was a thing of the past
but here's the thing—these Mondays!
These ecstatic drives while the sun sets
over our still-beating bodies!
I did not mean for this to be a love poem
but these things take their due course.
Like avalanches, like typhoons, like any other
natural disaster, love will make a way.

THERE'S BEER IN THIS POEM

I was not invited to beer parties in high school. I didn't even know who to ask to get invited to beer parties. And yes, it should say something about me that I called them *beer parties*. The closest I ever got to real high school debauchery was watching *Can't Hardly Wait* or eavesdropping in the girl's bathroom about how the foreign exchange student barfed upside down mid-keg stand. I will never know the thrill of underage drinking (only overage drinking). I'll never clonk plastic cups in the backyard of the soccer captain's house, someone's garage band playing a shitty rendition of "Freebird" on a makeshift stage. But the other problems of youth were still available to me: neck zits, pop quizzes, and saying the wrong thing in front of Bryan Buhro. I didn't have to go to a beer party to know just how gangly and repressed I was. The truth is, even if I had been invited, I probably wouldn't have gone. Would not have felt comfortable with the crowd of bodies undulating to pop music, boys leading girls upstairs by the hand. I'm not even sure these kinds of parties really exist, or if every movie from the 90s was just made to convince us we were all missing out on a central teenage experience. To attend a beer party. To watch sophomores throw up into bushes. To say the wrong thing in front of Bryan Buhro. And one hundred other people.

ALL MY FRIENDS ARE DEAD

Sometimes in the winter, I stand under pine trees
dropping their small caves & imagine
all my friends are dead. Some nuclear disaster
has befallen us, or they all had complications
due to alopecia. I'm all alone.

Kourtney would have wanted me to read
my tarot under the stars
the day of her funeral, Venus looking over
my solitary convention.
She would have made sure to supply
the place I chose with eucalyptus.

Jamie would not want me to grieve her,
but to drop my feelings into a cannon &
shoot them over a circus tent
in the pocket of the flying cannonball man.

Erica would be upset to know
I am even considering her death & would ask me
to stop writing this poem.

Sarah wouldn't be mad
when I stole a handful of her ashes
to brew into a cup of my favorite tea,
just to see what would happen.

When my mom dies, I'm planning on dropping
my whole basket—I've thought extensively about this.

Kristin has a bad encounter with an Airbnb host
& now her body is lost in the swamp.

Ali dies of old age, though the betting pool
had its odds on lung cancer or something really strange,
like mauled by bears.

And me—I'm left alone to contemplate this difficult news.

My friends dead. Every one of them.
The trees dropping down their cones
in the dark like bones. The clouds
moving slow over the parking lot sky.

WHAT TO LOOK FOR IN A HORSE

Get a horse with a little sass. One that will try
to buck you if she knows you've been drinking
too much. Get a horse with a pretty mane. They say
looks aren't everything, but they're wrong. Have
a horse that will look you square in the eye and say
Girl, what the fuck were you thinking last night?
Zach? Really? Your horse must be willing to trample
anyone who was mean to you in your childhood.
Be able to run faster than your sadness. It is not important
whether or not your horse can sing, or if she has a felony
record. In fact, a record in certain cases could be helpful.
Her flanks should feel smooth against your ankles,
keys sliding into soft ignitions. She must always be ready to run.

I WAS BORN SCREAMING AND I HAVE NEVER STOPPED

I was born on a Thursday, a small thing screaming
into the night. When I was two, my mom left me
alone in the high chair with my sister
and went to take a shower
and my sister bit both my feet, one after the other.
My mom ran naked out of the shower, hair wet,
big-bud nipples drooping in front of her children
and said *what the hell did you do?* My feet
were throbbing like in a cartoon, she said.
Why did you bite her? she said.
My sister looked my mom square in the eye
and said *because I love her.* But I know
it's because I was born a pain in the ass
and even a four-year-old knows you have to show
a pain in the ass who's boss.
I've been making noise ever since.
I fumbled my way through the blue-collar
trauma factory of childhood, said the wrong things
at the wrong times, got dismissed from altar-server duties
for drinking communion wine in the confession booth
with Jonathan Widmer. Kicked out of girl scout camp
for unstaking Melinda Veliquette's tent
in the middle of the night during a storm, during which
she blew into a pine tree.
I've always been the last one ready in the morning,
the girl who misplaces her shoes at the party,
and the one who needs you to spot
her a fiver at lunch. What I want to say is,
the boys in my life have said I'm too much
but in the end, there's no one there

to protect me
but me. I've always been my own protector
and I'm not about to start apologizing for it now.

SVÅR UPPLÖSNING

My boyfriend broke up with me and he changed
his profile picture of us to a picture of soup.

He keeps texting me, though. *I'm in IKEA*
and everything here makes me think of you.

He wants to have his breakup
and eat it too. Is he in the section with all the beds?

The food court? The parking lot?
What? I have so many questions.

It feels like an accomplishment
to be so linked to IKEA in likeness.

He misses me, he says. I say,
that's a very thin emotion.

ON THE EIGHTH DAY

But on the eighth day, God wakes up with a hangover
and can't find his tie. God wakes up with "Maneater"
stuck in his head and goes about his day doing
the dishes, fishing his keys out of his pocket to go buy
bread and softly singing to himself, *if you're in it for love,*
you ain't gonna get too far. On the ninth day God makes
pancakes and watches out over the little blue marble
he created and sees that things have already gone to shit.
But the pancakes were good. On the tenth day, rain.
On the eleventh day, backgammon. If God wears underwear,
he washes it on the twelfth day. By the end of week two,
God's on a lucky streak and he's taking money from the angels
left and right—Texas Hold'em. There's not a lot to do
in heaven but sit and watch, and the people are fucking
it up and God forgot to leave his number.
So on the sixteenth day he throws down a little dust
but they can't see the magic in it. They don't know
about music yet—it will take eons, and God
still has that fucking song stuck in his head.

READY TO ORDER

I am thrilled to announce that this is not
the first time I have been kicked out of Starbucks.

The customer is always right,
even if she doesn't know the answer

to *ma'am, are you going to buy something
or are you just going to cry?* What I want

is not listed anywhere on the menu.
I want to be a hot redhead on the hood

of a Jaguar in a Whitesnake video, ready
to fuck. I want to be a small deer or even

a dung beetle. I want to be a lost mitten collecting
snow under a streetlamp. I want all the minutes back

I spent on aborted hand jobs. I want to know
how it's possible to want so many things

and still want nothing.

THIS IS A SEX POEM

so you know you're going to be entertained.
There's probably gonna be something

in here about boobs and how I didn't want
to hook up with some guy because he plays

the trombone and that's not a sexy instrument.
I mean, just think about the way a trombone

sounds and then ask yourself I you want
to jump in the sack with a random guy from Tinder

named Sven who looks and sounds like THAT.
You don't. But this poem is about sex.

You did jump into the sack
with that trombone guy and the sex was Norwegian,

which means there was a minimal amount
of moaning. The Norwegians are notoriously

quiet. It's the Italians who are loud, and it's the guys
from Venezuela who tell you they want

to have your babies after they've spent
one night with you, and it's the Minnesota lesbians

who come to pick you up when your tire goes flat
on I-94 after coming home from the Twins game.

Guys named Zack will never call you back
and I've never met a good Matt

but Alisons have nice underwear and order you
Uber Eats without accepting compensation.

Patrick cries about his ex-lover
while you're still in his bed, and you feel weird

about it for six weeks
even though your therapist tell you not to

(you could sleep with your therapist
if you tried hard enough, but that would be weird).

There's always a Josh at the bar
willing to take you home, and a Dan is bad news—

but since this poem is about sex, go home.
Order yourself a taco

and tell yourself you're a bird.
See what happens.

CLIFFORD THE BIG RED DOG

My ex-boyfriend had a son who theorized
that Clifford the Big Red Dog is just
a normal-sized dog and all the people
in that town are super tiny. This was the most
exciting thing about my ex-boyfriend.
On a good day, he was half an inch taller than me
and he was the deli manager
at a high-end grocery store in Minnesota
which means that he knew a lot about cheese.
There were some nights we were a tangle
of arms, legs, hair. But what of it?
Nothing is better than his seven-year-old's
Clifford theory. Certainly not the dusty evening
I saw him struggle to change a tire
on the side of I-94, or the way he'd frantically
turn my boobs like a cartoon character
grabbing at spaceship knobs.
There isn't much to say about the fact
that we no longer speak except that
when I think of him, I think of a big, dumb dog
and a girl named Emily Elizabeth
who looks strangely like me.
And I wonder if she's sad, too.

THE SPEAKER OF THIS POEM IS LOOKING FOR A MAN

The speaker of this poem is willing to admit
      that her qualifications for a lover are many.
She's looking for a man who concedes
      that love is a risk. One who can draw
his gun quicker than she can draw hers.
      A man who was a fur trapper in a past life,
or at the very least a river bargeman
      with an untamable beard. She needs a man
who can lay himself down on the bed
      at the end of the day without a sigh.
He should keep a long list of losses
      pinned close to his breastbone.
The speaker of this poem seeks a man
      free of moles & genital warts.
A connoisseur of discount aisles, faraway
      laughter & birdcalls. The man should have
a box of ghosts. A love for pinball. The man
      should have an odd love for Pluto
that arose in 2006 after
      the International Astronomical Union
declared it was no longer a planet.
      Her man is a lover of the underdog
& the good-for-nothing.

A MAN IN THE BAR ASKS ME WHERE I'M FROM

and I spill my drink, lean forward to tell him I come
from the busted-ass oak trees of Ohio. I come from one-ply
toilet paper and mashed potatoes from a box.
I come from ash and ember, back roads and backhands,
an uncle lifting his niece up to see the fireworks
over the tree in the back of their trailer park. I come
from pain. I know dirt. I've planted flowers that never
came to blossom. And I come from music. From *Jesus
Christ Superstar* and my mom saving two years
to buy my first flute in the fourth grade. A *Gemeinhardt.*
I felt so rich I had to earn the breath it took to make it sing.
And I did. I come from loans and layaway.
I come from Faygo and farmland. A man once asked me
if I was redneck or hillbilly and I looked at him
and said boy, I'm a Master of Fine Arts.
I come from places you can't know, and it takes me
on my good legs to places green and bright.
I didn't come from tire swing, white fence, golden
retriever front yard. I come to you
with a drink in my hand asking to be heard.

ACKNOWLEDGMENTS

Thanks to the editors of the following magazines, where these poems first appeared, sometimes in different forms or with different titles:

Anti-Heroin Chic—"Seven Things"

Beloit Poetry Journal—"A Man in an Illinois Tollbooth Called Me a 'Beautiful Woman' As I Was Driving Away," "Svår Upplösning"

Copper Nickel—"Marrying the Wind"

MicroLit Almanac—"Party Tricks for a Sad Poet"

One Art—"How Gorilla Glue Couldn't Save My Marriage"

Smartish Pace—"Ten of Swords"

The Sun—"Almost Cha-Cha," "What to Look for in a Horse"

THANKS

Unending thanks to Courtney LeBlanc and Riot in Your Throat for publishing my first book. If you're reading this sentence, that means you're holding it. Which is unreal. It's been incredible.

I don't want to think about where I'd be now if it weren't for Erica Anderson-Senter, Sarah Sandman, and Kourtney Jones—in many ways, each the kite string and the kite. Thanks for being there when a good deal of these poems were written, and thanks for your tireless support and patience. For the late nights on the porch and at Camptown—I'm forever indebted.

To the class of Oh-Ten at Bennington College and the nights we spent at the End of the World, thank you. It was the best decision I ever made. And to Ed Ochester, Susan Kinsolving, Amy Gerstler, and Timothy Liu, who taught me more than I deserved to know. And who fought for me every step of the way.

Thanks to Desireé Dallagiacomo for welcoming me into the chaos and sweetness of Undercurrent, Throughline, and Kin Keeping. Desireé kept so many of us buoyant during the thickness and seclusion of 2020, and without her, I would not have written many of the poems in this book.

Del Doughty deserves a special mention, since I would not have gone to grad school or maybe even become a poet if it had not been for his aloof urging. Thank you, thank you. I hope you're having the best day of your life.

ABOUT THE AUTHOR

Brett Elizabeth Jenkins lives and writes in Fort Wayne, Indiana. She has an MFA from the Bennington Writers Seminars in Vermont and has published in magazines such as *The Sun*, *AGNI*, *Mid-American Review*, and *Beloit Poetry Journal*. *Brilliant Little Body* is her first full-length collection.

ABOUT THE PRESS

Riot in Your Throat is an independent press that
publishes fierce, feminist poetry.

Support independent authors, artists, and presses.

Visit us online:

www.riotinyourthroat.com